1993

Scheduling The Middle Level School

To Meet Early Adolescent Needs

By Ronald Williamson

National Association of Secondary School Principals

Ronald Williamson is former executive director for curriculum and instruction for the Ann Arbor (Mich.) Public Schools. He is now executive director of the National Middle Schools Association, Columbus, Ohio.

Copyright 1993
National Association of Secondary School Principals
1904 Association Dr., Reston, Va. 22091-1537
(703) 860-0200

Executive Director: Timothy J. Dyer
Associate Executive Director/Director of Middle Level Services: Laurel Martin Kanthak
Director of Publications and Marketing: Robert Mahaffey
Editor: Patricia George
Technical Editor: Eugenia Cooper Potter

ISBN: 0-88210-279-6
Printed in the U.S.A.

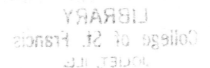

Contents

Appendices

Preface

How many times have you heard the phrase "it's a great idea but you can't schedule it"? This comment is often made when middle level educators talk about restructuring the school day and reorganizing the way instruction is delivered to students.

Building and implementing a school master schedule is one of the least exciting tasks of a school administrator. Yet, the scheduling of staff and students is perhaps one of the most critical tasks, due in part to the impact the schedule has on the structure and quality of the school day. The master schedule can either create opportunity or place barriers in the way of more effectively serving students.

This is especially true in the middle level school, where renewed focus on the learning characteristics of early adolescents has led many middle level schools to examine the ways in which students and staff are organized for instruction.

The implementation of teaching teams in the middle level school necessitates a reexamination of scheduling practices. The creation of blocks of time that may be used by the teaching teams greatly enhances the instructional flexibility and responsiveness of the teams.

This monograph has two purposes. First, it will discuss and offer suggestions regarding the development and implementation of a master schedule. Second, it will address the concepts and offer models for the scheduling of flexible blocks of time. It is this second purpose that has the greater potential for significantly affecting the daily life of students.

The challenge confronting the administrator in implementing a block-time schedule is similar to that addressed with other issues: assisting the staff in taking the risk to "do business differently for kids." It is a worthy challenge and one that must be taken as the middle level school strives to reach its full potential.

Ron Williamson

1 Middle Level Students

EARLY adolescence is a time of tremendous change: physical, social, emotional, and intellectual. Joan Lipsitz, author of *Successful Schools for Young Adolescents* (1984), says that more changes take place during this time than during any other, except the time from birth to age three.

While adolescence is marked by profound changes in physical appearance, the age at which the changes take place varies widely. While not universally true, girls generally mature earlier than boys. This maturity difference accounts for some of the changes in social interaction between boys and girls that occur at this age.

Changes in metabolism, heart beat, blood pressure, and pulse, due in part to tremendous physical growth that takes place during adolescence, cause students to be energetic and restless one moment and listless the next.

The onset of puberty in both boys and girls means that students become increasingly sensitive to and yet often intolerant of the sexual maturation they are experiencing. Changes in voice and the appearance of body hair and other secondary sex characteristics often leave the middle level student uneasy and extremely self-conscious.

Middle level students who look as though they belong in a high school are seated adjacent to youngsters whose feet barely reach the floor.

While physical growth and maturation are the most obvious of the developmental changes, the area that perhaps is most confounding to parents and educators is the change in students' social and emotional development.

During the middle grades, students increasingly seek independence from adults and conformity to peers. They both strive for independence yet seek guidance. They need personal attention from adults, yet seek conformity to their peer group.

Middle level students are often overly concerned about the way they are perceived by others, particularly their peers. They are playing to an "imaginary audience." For example, when a student trips going up the stairs, the most common reaction is to look around and see if anyone is watching.

In their quest to achieve acceptance, adolescents often overcompensate and seek conformity in dress, hair style, music, and other indicators of the peer culture.

1

While adolescents are striving for increasing independence, most report positive relationships with their parents. Joan Lipsitz and Gayle Dorman (Lipsitz, 1984) cite evidence that while many disagreements between parents and students occur during the middle school years, the primary issue seems to be one of the family adjusting to the rapid developmental changes of the adolescent rather than the strife and dissension of a child rebelling against family beliefs or practices.

While the changes in the intellectual realm are less visible, they often rival the rapid physical growth in importance as they, too, affect both social and emotional development.

In early adolescence, youngsters begin to move away from the almost complete reliance on their own concrete experiences and toward the ability to consider alternatives. The ability to develop hypotheses, to consider "what if's," to think reflectively, and to reason abstractly characterize this period. As in the other areas of development, the changes do not take place in a linear progression but often surface in fits and starts. One day a youngster will be able to deal with complex abstract concepts and the next day will once again require instruction in the most concrete manner.

The challenge for the teacher is to adjust the instructional program to take into account the students' differences in cognitive development—the differences from student to student and from day to day.

In addition to great variety in learning styles and thinking abilities, the interests of early adolescents change frequently. They are curious and interested in trying many different activities. This change in interests also affects the instructional program and the structure of lessons taught at the middle level.

In addition, due to a combination of factors such as peer pressure and self-esteem, many early adolescents voluntarily suppress their own academic achievement. Some students at the middle level, quite capable of high academic achievement, choose to perform at a lower level, fearful that if they achieve "too well" in school, they will not be accepted by their peers.

Summary

Adolescence is a wonderful time, a time of profound change for youngsters as they make the adjustment from childhood to adulthood. It is the time when most students experience significant physical growth and become increasingly concerned about their appearance and social connections.

While adolescents' physical growth is most apparent, the social and emotional changes, as well as the cognitive changes, are equally important. Adolescents are increasingly concerned about their connection to the peer group, seek greater independence from adults, and require frequent opportunities to experience success. As adolescents change intellectually, they begin to be able to deal with abstract concepts instead of operating solely in the concrete realm.

However, the most important consideration in adolescent development is the great diversity among students. No two adolescents are exactly alike. This diversity is the basis of the middle level program and responsiveness to adolescent development is the hallmark of a quality middle level experience.

REFERENCES

Berla, Nancy; Henderson, Anne T.; and Kerewsky, William. *The Middle School Years—A Parent's Handbook.* Columbia, Md.: National Committee for Citizens in Education, 1989.

Elkind, David. *The Hurried Child.* Reading, Mass.: Addison-Wesley, 1981.

Lipsitz, Joan. *Successful Schools for Young Adolescents.* New Brunswick, N.J.: Transaction Books, 1984.

Lounsbury, John; Mariani, Jean; and Compton, Mary. *The Middle School in Profile: A Day in the Seventh Grade.* Columbus, Ohio: National Middle School Association, 1980.

Milgram, Joel. "The Sixth Grader: A Profile." In *Life in the Three Sixth Grades,* edited by John Lounsbury and J. Howard Johnston. Reston, Va.: National Association of Secondary School Principals, 1988.

————. "The Eighth Grader: A Profile." In *Inside Grade Eight.* Reston, Va.: National Association of Secondary School Principals, 1990.

————. "The Ninth Grade: A Profile." In *How Fares the Ninth Grade.* Reston, Va.: National Association of Secondary School Principals, 1985.

2 Scheduling: Issues and Considerations

MIDDLE level schools must respond to the developmental needs of their students. The degree to which a school responds is influenced by the structure of the school schedule.

For example, understanding that middle level students begin to think abstractly at different times may affect a school's grouping practices. The rapid physical changes that take place during adolescence means that students are often restless and have a short attention span. Structuring a schedule to ensure frequent opportunities for movement will greatly enhance the school's ability to respond to student needs.

Preparing a middle level school schedule can be tedious and time-consuming, particularly if administrators see it as a test of their management skills. However, scheduling *can* be an opportunity to address goals, promote innovation, strengthen problem-solving skills, and better serve the middle level student.

Scheduling can be broken into four distinct phases:

1. Planning and preparing
2. Collecting data
3. Developing the schedule
4. Implementing the schedule.

Scheduling is a vital function for middle level administrators for several reasons.

First, the schedule is a tool to serve students. The structure of the student day and the ease with which students are able to access a school's curricular program may be either helped or hindered by the school schedule.

The schedule also promotes a particular philosophy about the way teachers and students interact, and either creates opportunity for improved service to students or creates hurdles that inhibit the instructional program.

Scheduling also promotes delivery of the curriculum and addresses the instructional needs of staff and students. The schedule determines whether or not all students are able to have equal access to curriculum offerings.

For example, many effective middle level programs organize teachers and students into interdisciplinary teams. Teams of two or more teachers share students and ideally have classrooms located adjacent to each other, have common planning time, and have similar teaching schedules.

5

In scheduling elective classes, placement of band, choir, and foreign language offerings determines whether or not all students who wish to take a course are able to do so. For example, if all eighth graders may elect to take band, but band is scheduled at a time when one team of eighth graders is in core classes, it may be impossible for those students to have access to the band course. One solution may be to not place band students on this team. However, doing so would raise other scheduling concerns such as the grouping of students.

Since the structure of a master schedule can have such a significant impact on a school's program, all the items that define the local parameters for the school's schedule must be identified prior to developing the schedule.

The most important consideration is the stated mission or philosophy of the middle level school. The school's schedule must provide a structure in which both students and teachers can achieve the mission. For example, attention to the developmental needs of middle level students may require a review of the structure and time allotment for the lunch period or to the length and/or sequence of classes.

In addition, a middle level school with a teaming or advisory program will want to structure the day so the teams share schedules and common planning time and ensure that advisory is scheduled to promote the program's objectives.

While the stated mission of the school and the programmatic components of a school should be the primary focus of a school schedule, administrators must consider other local parameters and guidelines as well. These include bus schedule, physical plant, length of the school day, and contractual conditions of employment for teachers and other staff members. These factors do not function in isolation; they interact with each other. This interconnectedness challenges administrators developing the schedule.

Develop a Plan

February is generally an appropriate time to develop the plan, detail the timeline, and prepare materials for use with staff, students, and parents.

A scheduling plan should include steps to address several issues: parent and student orientation, the course selection process, staff member involvement in determining scheduling priorities, the timeline for schedule simulations, and a process for finalizing and distributing individual student and teacher schedules.

Timelines can list each part of the scheduling plan along with the date on which the step is to occur. Using a calendar such as the model included in Appendix A allows the administrator to carefully monitor each step of the scheduling process.

When developing the timeline, several items must be considered: classroom visits to talk with students, parent information sessions, modification and printing of course selection materials, accountability for each component of the plan, and training for those involved in each step of the scheduling plan.

Scheduling goals also provide a focus for the scheduling plan if selected early in the process. Two examples of scheduling goals might be:

1. All students will be scheduled by the end of the school year.

2. All staff members will be notified of their tentative assignments by the end of the school year.

Goals such as these are very attainable. Realistic planning and careful implementation of the plan will help to ensure accomplishment.

Scheduling involves gathering and processing immense amounts of information. Determining the information needs and gathering the data prior to scheduling are important first steps.

A list of elementary school students who will be moving to the school will allow the middle level administrator to become familiar with incoming students. Administrators must know which students qualify for special services such as reading support or special education, for example. Data regarding the ethnic and socioeconomic status of all students helps provide balance to all classes.

Middle level administrators will also want to ensure that all incoming students have enrolled and selected classes prior to the assignment of staff, because the number of teachers assigned to the school and to particular classes frequently depends on student enrollment.

A list of teachers, room numbers, courses offered, student numbers, and the number of students electing each course also assist the administrator in constructing the schedule.

Schools utilizing a computer to manage the scheduling task must continually update the computer files to ensure the accuracy of the course table and student files.

Establish Scheduling Priorities

Establishing scheduling priorities is one of the most important scheduling activities, yet it is also one of the easiest to overlook. Middle level administrators must determine what they wish to accomplish, what programs they want to facilitate, and what goals they want to meet via the master schedule.

The school schedule is a powerful tool for managing a school. Once a schedule begins to take shape it is difficult to modify. Therefore, school priorities to be achieved through the master schedule must be detailed early in the process.

The central question is: What does a school want to accomplish through the master schedule? Such issues as implementing common planning time, block scheduling, teaming arrangements, and an adviser/advisee program fit into this category. Determining priorities before constructing a schedule provides an opportunity to develop a schedule that addresses identified needs. Hoping that priorities will be met "by chance" can lead to frustration. Setting priorities at an early date and working to make them happen can be rewarding.

Summary

Effective middle level schedules are flexible and responsive to student needs and are based on a stated philosophy and goals. The needs of students and the program drive the development of the schedule. Ensuring the inclusion of blocks of instructional time, appropriate planning time for staff members, advisory time, flexibility for special schedules, and providing for the needs of both elective and core programs are examples of factors that guide the development of a middle level schedule.

REFERENCES

Clark, Sally N., and Clark, Donald C. "Restructuring Middle Schools: Strategies for Using *Turning Points.*" *Schools in the Middle*, December 1990.

Dempsey, Richard, and Traverso, Henry. *Scheduling the Secondary School.* Reston, Va.: National Association of Secondary School Principals, 1983.

Toepfer, Conrad F. "Middle Level School Grades and Program Development." *Schools in the Middle*, April 1990.

3 The Flexible Block-Time Schedule

THE term "flexible schedule" may at first be considered an oxymoron. How can one develop and adhere to a schedule and at the same time provide flexibility?

Flexibility in a schedule is as much an attitude as a concept. While the ideal schedule might allow every teacher in every course and content area total flexibility in providing for the instructional needs of students, reality of managing a middle level school quickly establishes parameters that impinge on total flexibility.

The term "flexible scheduling" refers here to arranging classes to permit the instructional staff to alter or modify the schedule on a daily basis.

Flexible scheduling is a way to respond to the diverse needs of middle level students. For example, it permits teachers and students to vary the routine and location of classes. When I taught on a middle school interdisciplinary team, our team schedule had a four class period block that extended from 8:30 a.m. until noon. During that time, four content areas were taught. The team varied the schedule by rotating the order of classes. During each month, the arrangement of classes was modified. As a result of this flexibility, students responded differently to the content being presented based on the time of the day.

As a teacher, I know I am at my best early in the day. Students who routinely have me for instruction late in the day are not receiving the same quality of instruction as the morning students. Having the flexibility to respond to both student and teacher needs is another benefit of a flexible schedule.

Since flexibility is an attitude, it is a concept that does not lend itself to implementation by administrative fiat. Implementation requires two steps:

1. Develop a schedule that provides a structure and opportunities for flexibility.
2. Work with staff members to ensure utilization of the flexibility built into the schedule. Achieving the full potential of a flexible schedule is perhaps the greatest hurdle to implementation.

Blocks of Time

The most frequent model for providing flexibility in the middle level schedule is establishing blocks of time for teaching teams. This concept is closely linked to the establishment of interdisciplinary teams: two or more teachers who share students. A team may or may not have a similar schedule; however, scheduling all teachers on a team with the same schedule provides opportunities to increase the flexibility of the instructional program.

To illustrate this point, let's assume the team consists of four eighth grade teachers: language arts, mathematics, science, and social studies. The team is scheduled with its students during first and second hour, and fifth and sixth hour each day. In our example, each class period is 45 minutes in length, which provides this team with two blocks of time—one in the morning and one in the afternoon—that are 90 minutes in length.

Class Period	
1	BLOCK
2	BLOCK
3	
4	
5	BLOCK
6	BLOCK
7	

Many different models provide blocks of time for teachers. While there is no conclusive evidence about the relative advantages and disadvantages of two, three, or four-period blocks, building a schedule that provides blocks of time facilitates the work of teams in adjusting their instructional program to respond more effectively to students.

One note of caution: Establishing blocks of time does not ensure that teams will utilize the flexibility inherent in such a model. However, without the structure that provides the blocks, it is nearly impossible for a teaching team to adjust their time use.

Advantages and Disadvantages of Block Time

As with any instructional practice, there are both pros and cons to providing flexibility in the schedule. The relative strength of the rationale will be influenced by the administrators', teachers', and students' role in the middle level school and their beliefs about middle level education.

Administrators. Flexible scheduling can both enhance the development of a middle level program and provide an additional burden. For an administrator, the schedule is a visible indicator of the priorities and goals of the middle level school. The flexibility of that schedule provides a structure in which the middle level teacher may refine and enhance their instructional practices to respond to students needs.

The block-time schedule also simplifies the scheduling process. Once a student is assigned to a team and that team is allotted blocks of time for instruction, the team assumes the responsibility for detailing the use of that time. The administrator, however, must ensure that there are no irresolvable conflicts among the various team blocks.

For the most part, the advantages of the block-time schedule rest on philosophical and programmatic grounds; the disadvantages are primarily related to logistics. Implementation of a block-time schedule complicates the scheduling of itinerant staff, use of part-time staff, scheduling of pull-out programs, and the lunch hour. However, these factors are hurdles common to the construction of nearly all schedules.

Administrators may also encounter resistance from opponents of a flexible schedule who raise concerns about protecting academic time, time for specific content areas, and preparing students for the structure of the high school day.

The conflict is related to the school's mission. On one hand is the need to ensure that middle level students receive a challenging, enriched, and intense academic program to prepare them for life in the next century. On the other hand is the desire to ensure that adolescents receive instruction in an environment that responds to their developmental needs and reflects an understanding of the variables that promote increased student achievement.

Open dialog among staff members and administrators enhances the school's ability to ensure a common vision for the students in the middle level program. A flexible schedule can provide a challenging academic program and be responsive to students.

Teachers. The primary responsibility for implementing a block-time schedule rests with the teachers, because once the master schedule provides options for flexibility, the teachers must utilize the available options.

In addition to responding to student developmental needs, the flexible schedule provides several advantages for teachers:

- It permits variation in length of time allotted to individual subjects based on teacher and student need.
- It allows teachers and students to teach and learn according to their learning style preference for morning or afternoon.
- It provides options for scheduling special activities such as assemblies, team meetings, or field trips and still permits each student to meet with each teacher during the day.
- It provides opportunities to group and regroup students without totally reorganizing classes or tracking.
- It provides options for team teachers to correlate subject matter and engage in interdisciplinary instruction.
- It permits the instructional staff to organize students to provide both large and small-group instruction.

One of the disadvantages of flexible scheduling is that it is not easily understood, especially among new students, parents, and substitute teachers.

On a flexible schedule, team teachers must share the same block of time to meet, talk, and plan together. Successful utilization of a flexible schedule requires commitment to collaborative planning. Some teachers see this team planning as detracting from their own individual planning time. Continued discussion of this issue most often leads to resolution.

Another perceived disadvantage of flexible scheduling is the perception that teaming in general, and block-of-time scheduling specifically, detract from a teacher's freedom of action. In addition, conflicts between teachers may arise regarding the use of time. Implementing a flexible schedule requires that teachers have cooperative planning skills.

Some teachers may be reluctant to endorse a flexible scheduling option due to their unfamiliarity with the concept or their own insecurity about change. Open discussion of the issues, including the articulation of specific scheduling models, often helps them overcome much of this anxiety.

Students. Flexible scheduling provides middle level students with many of the advantages and disadvantages mentioned for administrators and teachers.

As the schedule and instructional practices become increasingly responsive to the developmental needs of students, the opportunity for students to reach their full potential increases. Correlating content across subject matter lines, grouping and regrouping students for instruction, adjusting the time allotment for content areas, facilitating the scheduling of assemblies and special activities, and modifying the routine of the day all enhance student achievement and a student's sense of efficacy.

Flexibility Other Than Block-Time Schedules

As middle level schools adopt an instructional model built around interdisciplinary teams, the concept of blocks of time is often used to provide flexibility. However, other models also utilize flexibility, including the use of alternate day classes, rotating schedules, and dropped classes.

Alternate Day Classes. The use of alternate day classes permits students to attend more classes than there are class periods. For example, students might be scheduled for both physical education and foreign language during the same class period. The two courses meet on alternate days, every other day throughout the school year.

The alternate day scheduling pattern permits teachers in two content areas to correlate their subject matter, group or regroup students for specific instruction, and combine classes for particular activities.

Other alternate day rotations may include art and chorus, foreign language and performing arts, or technology education and computers. The combinations are limitless.

Rotating Schedules. An advantage of block time scheduling is the ability to rotate classes so students and teachers can work together at various times during the day. This is an example of a rotating schedule—the rotation of content areas within the interdisciplinary team.

The entire school schedule can also be rotated. Such a rotation provides opportunities for every student and every teacher to benefit, although such a rotation also poses some logistical problems related to use of itinerant and part-time staff.

FIGURE 1

ROTATING SCHEDULE

Monday	Tuesday	Wednesday	Thursday	Friday
1	7	6	5	2
2	1	7	6	3
3	2	1	7	4
4	3	2	1	5
5	4	3	2	6
6	5	4	3	7
7	6	5	4	1

As Figure 1 demonstrates, the schedule rotates every day. Thus, the day begins and ends at a different point in the rotation.

This concept may be enhanced when the concept of a rotating schedule is combined with the block-time concept for teams. For example, assume that the team has block time for four class periods: first, second, fifth, and sixth. Impose the blocks on the rotating schedule and the blocks rotate throughout the day.

The nature of the rotation and the length of the blocks affect the structure of the day for both teachers and students. Some blocks will be longer, some shorter; some will be in the morning, others in the afternoon. Combining the two concepts maximizes the potential for flexibility in the schedule. However, the schedule may become too flexible, too variable, and resistance to the model may overwhelm the commitment to flexibility. (See Figure 2)

FIGURE 2

ROTATING SCHEDULE

Monday	Tuesday	Wednesday	Thursday	Friday
1	7	6	5	2
2	1	7	6	3
3	2	1	7	4
4	3	2	1	5
5	4	3	2	6
6	5	4	3	7
7	6	5	4	1

Dropped Schedule. This scheduling concept is built on the premise that not every course needs to meet every day of the week. Students may be scheduled for more classes than there are class periods. On any given day, one of the courses will be dropped. Figure 3 illustrates the concept.

FIGURE 3

ROTATING DROPPED SCHEDULE

Monday	Tuesday	Wednesday	Thursday	Friday
1	8	1	1	1
2	2	2	2	2
3	3	8	3	3
4	4	4	8	4
5	5	5	5	8
6	6	6	6	6
7	7	7	7	7

In this example, every student has eight classes, but only seven meet on any day. One class is dropped in order to add the eighth class.

This option is utilized by some schools to provide a scheduling alternative for the advisory program, for sustained silent reading or sustained silent writing, assemblies or special activities, study skills instruction, or other local options.

Examples of Flexible Schedules

Flexible block-time schedules come in many variations. Every schedule is developed based on local resources and guidelines. The following schedules provide examples of the issues that may be addressed with a flexible schedule. They should be reviewed for the concepts addressed and their respective advantages and disadvantages. None of the models are ideal flexible schedules or should be replicated exactly in every middle level school.

Example 1. *Description:* This model comes from a 6–8 school that has three small units or houses. Each house is a grade. House A is composed of sixth graders, house B of seventh graders, and house C of eighth graders.

This schedule provides academic blocks throughout the day. While most blocks are at least two class hours in length, it is necessary to have blocks of shorter duration for one group of students. The schedule has been structured to provide an advisory period at the beginning of the day that permits students to begin their day with their adviser and ensures the adviser has an opportunity to gauge how students are doing as they enter the school.

EXAMPLE 1: Flexible Schedule

A	B	C
ADVISORY	ADVISORY	ADVISORY
BLOCK	ELECTIVE	BLOCK
	BLOCK	ELECTIVE
ELECTIVE		BLOCK
LUNCH	ELECTIVE	ELECTIVE
BLOCK	LUNCH	ELECTIVE
	BLOCK	LUNCH
EXPLORATORY		BLOCK
EXPLORATORY	ELECTIVE	

The location of the blocks provides opportunity for cross-graded courses. Electives can be shared between students in groups B and C, while students may be grouped between and among the three groups for block classes. This creates opportunities for the flexible advancement of students and for some grouping and regrouping of students for instruction.

Example 2. *Description:* This schedule from a middle level school in western Michigan provides variety in the daily schedule. Some of the core classes—social studies, science, communications, physical education, and unified arts—meet four days each week. This allows the scheduling of mini-courses.

Each Monday is a base day: mini-courses are not offered. Tuesday has the same schedule as Monday, except mini-courses are offered in place of the seventh hour class.

On Wednesday, the rotating schedule takes effect. The 7th period class dropped on Tuesday is taught first period on Wednesday, with the first period class taught second period, the second period class taught third period, etc. On Wednesday, the 7th period class is dropped for mini-courses and taught first period on Thursday.

Performing music and basic skills are offered everyday—second period for sixth grade, third period for seventh grade, and fourth period for eighth grade. This part of the schedule is not affected by the rotating schedule.

EXAMPLE 2: Flexible Schedule

6th Grade

	1	2	3	4	5	6	7
Monday	M		U	SS	S	P	C
Tuesday	M		U	SS	S	P	MC
Wednesday	C		M	U	SS	S	MC
Thursday	P		C	M	U	SS	MC
Friday	S		P	C	M	U	MC

7th Grade

	1	2	3	4	5	6	7
Monday	M	U		SS	S	P	C
Tuesday	M	U		SS	S	P	MC
Wednesday	C	M		U	SS	S	MC
Thursday	P	C		M	U	SS	MC
Friday	S	P		C	M	U	MC

8th Grade

	1	2	3	4	5	6	7
Monday	M	U	SS		S	P	C
Tuesday	M	U	SS		S	P	MC
Wednesday	C	M	U		SS	S	MC
Thursday	P	C	M		U	SS	MC
Friday	S	P	C		M	U	MC

M Mathematics
U Unified Arts
   Shop
   Art
   Home Economics
   Computer Lab
   Robotics
   Planetarium
   Music Lab
SS Social Studies
S Science
P Physical Education
C Communicating
MC Mini-courses

Daily Schedule

8:00	Students Enter School
8:10- 8:55	1st Hour
8:55- 9:40	2nd Hour
9:40-10:25	3rd Hour
10:25-11:10	4th Hour
11:10-11:55	5th Hour
11:55-12:00	Rotate to Homeroom Area
12:00-12:15	Lunch
12:15-12:45	Student Recess
12:45-12:50	Pass in Class
12:50- 1:35	6th Hour
1:35- 2:30	7th Hour

EXAMPLE 3: Flexible Schedule

House 6
CORE BLOCK (2) + ADVISORY
ELECTIVE OR EXPLORATORY (ROTATION 1)
LUNCH
CORE BLOCK (2)
EXPLORATORY (ROTATION 1 & 2)
ELECTIVE OR EXPLORATORY (ROTATION 2)

Gold House 7/8 Morning

ELECTIVE
CORE BLOCK (2) + ADVISORY
ELECTIVE

Red House 7/8 Morning

ELECTIVE
CORE BLOCK (2) + ADVISORY
ELECTIVE

All 7th Graders Afternoon

LUNCH
CORE BLOCK (2)
ELECTIVE

All 8th Graders Afternoon

ELECTIVE
LUNCH
CORE BLOCK (2)

Example 3. *Description:* This example comes from a Michigan middle level school (6–8) composed of three small houses. One house has sixth grade, while the other two houses have both seventh and eighth graders. This schedule has many of the advantages described for the first example: blocks throughout the school day, opportunities for cross-graded electives and core classes, and the potential for flexible grouping and regrouping of students.

However, this schedule is structured so all seventh graders have the same schedule in the afternoon. All eighth graders also have a common schedule. This variation on the schedule provides greater opportunity for the scheduling of classes that are offered only to one particular grade, and also permits students to eat lunch with their grade level group.

Example 4. *Description:* This scheduling model is used in a Texas middle level school. The school has an eight-period day with one of the periods serving as a combination lunch period and study hall. This school utilizes a variation of the rotating schedule that schedules individual courses at different places in the day depending on the day of the week. Third, fourth, and fifth hours are held constant. Third period is used

EXAMPLE 4: Flexible Schedule

	Monday	Tuesday	Wednesday	Thursday	Friday
8:30– 9:20	1	8	7	6	2
9:25–10:10	2	1	8	7	6
10:15–11:05	3	3	3	3	3
11:10–12:00	4	4	4	4	4
12:05–12:55	5	5	5	5	5
1:00– 1:45	6	2	1	8	7
1:50– 2:35	7	6	2	1	8
2:40– 3:30	8	7	6	2	1

for attendance for state reporting purposes, while fourth and fifth hours are used for lunch periods.

Such a schedule permits teachers and students to work together at different times during the day. This rotating schedule ensures that sometime during the week, students will be in a class early in the day or late in the day. This allows students and staff members to gain an enhanced perspective about each other.

For example, the student who may be inattentive and disengaged at the end of the day may be enthusiastic and involved in the morning. Likewise, teachers who are at their best in the morning will be permitted to work with all students during their prime time.

In addition, the rotating schedule ensures that disruptions that routinely occur in one part of the day, such as the late arrival of buses or early dismissal for sporting events, will not always affect the same class.

EXAMPLE 5: Exploratory Schedule

1st Quarter	2nd Quarter	3rd Quarter	4th Quarter
Art	Home Economics	Technology Education	Drama
Exploratory Foreign Language		Computers	General Music

Example 5. *Description:* This schedule includes exploratory classes scheduled during two consecutive class periods. Students rotate through the exploratory classes during the school year. For example, students who have art during the first quarter have home economics during the second quarter, technology education during the third quarter, and drama for the fourth quarter. In addition, the same student groups are assigned to classes during both hours. That is, students in art and home economics one hour are in exploratory foreign language the second hour. Students in technology education are also in computers.

This permits the exploratory teachers to share students and provides a schedule that meets some of the criteria for teaming. Teachers are able to correlate curriculum across the content areas and develop common practices and procedures for all exploratory classes.

Another important benefit of this schedule is that it allows the exploratory team—either the entire group, or a subset such as drama and general music—to treat the two hours as a block of time and to adjust the length of the classes to meet the needs of students or the needs of the curriculum.

EXAMPLE 6: Flexible Schedule

	Monday	Tuesday	Wednesday	Thursday	Friday
1	Core	Elective	Elective	Core	Core
2		Core	Core	Elective	
3	Elective			Core	
4	Elective		Elective		Elective
5	Core	Elective	Core	Elective	Core
6		Core		Core	
7					Elective

19

Example 6. *Description:* Every day of the week is different from every other day both in the location of courses and the length of the blocks of time provided for core teams. The school has a seven-period day and lunch is scheduled either between third and fourth period or between fourth and fifth period. The illustrated schedule is for only one of the grades in the school.

The core subjects of mathematics, language arts, science, and social studies are taught by a team of teachers who have a common schedule. The instructional blocks of time provided for this team vary both in length and in placement during the day.

On Monday, the team has a two-period block in the morning and a three-period block in the afternoon; on Tuesday there is a three-hour block in the morning and a two-period block in the afternoon. On Thursday the team has two, two-hour blocks—one morning and one afternoon—and a single class period early in the day. This provides the team with great flexibility in arranging their instructional periods and many options for grouping and regrouping students.

The elective courses are also scheduled at various times during the school day. When the schedules for all three grades are developed, it is possible to align certain periods so in performing music and other courses, students can be assembled for ensembles and other groups without disrupting the remainder of the schedule. A major disadvantage of this scheduling model is the complexity of scheduling if staff members are shared between and among schools, which is often the case for teachers of elective courses.

This model provides a great deal of flexibility in the day. However, it also requires substantial commitment from the teaching staff. The model challenges most of the standards for the development of a middle level schedule: classes of a standard length located in a fixed time slot each day of the week.

Considerations and Local Parameters

The size of the school, the number of students and teachers, the number of teachers shared with another school, class size requirements, capacity of the lunch room, grouping policies, contractual requirements, and starting and ending times all affect the school schedule.

A middle school principal in Michigan recently distributed a memo to her staff that delineated all the parameters affecting her ability to create the "ideal" schedule. Several of the considerations described in the memo demonstrate the complexity of developing a flexible block-time schedule. (The complete text of the memo is included in Appendix B.):

- Time parameters: Begin at 8:05, end at 2:45, 25-minute advisory, seven 45-minute classes, 5 minutes passing time, three lunch periods of 30 minutes each.
- No teacher may teach more than 200 minutes in a row without a lunch break or planning period.
- No more than two-thirds of the students may be in electives at any one time because there are not enough classes to accommodate them.
- Two orchestras must be scheduled consecutively due to part-time teacher.

- Seventh and eighth graders must have two common elective periods to accommodate singleton electives open to students in both grades.

Every school will have its own set of constraints and parameters. Prior to developing the schedule it is important to identify all the factors that will either restrain or enhance the development of a schedule.

Conditions for Success

Several factors contribute to the success of the program. While each of the factors does not in and of itself either promote or hinder success, as a group they greatly enhance the likelihood for smooth implementation.

Administrative Support. One of the most important components of any change effort is the leadership provided by the administrator. The administrator's advocacy for a new direction, sensitivity to the issues of change, and ability to provide the resources to support a new endeavor all affect the degree of acceptance of new programs. These factors certainly contribute to the success of a flexible scheduling option.

In most schools, the middle level administrator is responsible for developing the schedule and for working with the staff members to develop an implementation model that is appropriate for that school site. Therefore, it is the administrator who must be knowledgeable about effective middle level practices such as block-time scheduling.

Thorough Planning. Traditionally, the middle level school day has been composed of a series of equal-length class periods. Students move from classroom to classroom at an established time, signaled by the ringing of a bell.

Adopting a flexible scheduling model means modifying this traditional school organization. One implication is the reduction of standard-length class periods and the attendant movement of the entire student body in the hallways several times during the school day. Since all classes may not be the same length or meet at the same time, another implication may be the reduction or elimination of the bell to signal the beginning and end of class periods.

Each of these changes may require modifying the very culture of the middle level school. Teachers, parents, students, and even the middle level administrator may only be familiar with the traditional organizational patterns. Modifying these cultural norms will require sufficient planning and discussion of all the implications of such a change.

Adequate planning includes creating a common information base about the current conditions and the rationale for a modified structure, involving all school constituencies in the development of a scheduling model, and attending to the needs of all constituencies to be informed about the modified structure. These and other aspects of program planning are discussed in detail in NASSP's *Planning for Success: Successful Implementation of Middle Level Reorganization* (1991).

Flexible Space. While not a prerequisite for implementation of a flexible schedule, the availability of both small and large group meeting areas will facilitate such a schedule. One of the major benefits of a flexible schedule is the ability to group and regroup students, to meet in various size groups, and to organize students in groups that are most effective instructionally. Each of these activities is enhanced by the availability of flexible space.

Staff Support. Creating a flexible schedule is just the first step in providing options for the use of instructional time. Middle level administrators must support the teachers as they implement a flexible model. This support includes several components.

First, administrators must provide appropriate training to help the teachers develop an understanding of the concept, become familiar with the advantages and disadvantages of the model, and work with their colleagues to develop activities and models that take advantage of a flexible schedule.

Second, administrators can heighten dissonance regarding current practices by gathering data regarding current practices, providing information to shape attitudes, and developing models that demonstrate the modified practices.

Third, administrators must recognize that while some teachers will enthusiastically implement a flexible schedule, others will resist until it is clear that the model will be successful.

Fourth, administrators must help teachers respond to the questions of parents and others, such as "How do you ensure that the curriculum is being taught?" and "Does this meet all the state requirements for minutes of instruction?"

Summary

Ensuring flexibility in the instructional day is a worthy goal for the middle level school, as it illustrates sensitivity to and responsiveness to the developmental needs of middle level students.

Implementing a schedule that provides flexibility is not easy. It requires a discussion of the concept, the development of a foundation of rationale among the staff, and creative problem solving in addressing the logistical issues associated with creation of a schedule.

No one model for flexibility has greater advantages than any other. As with most aspects of the educational process, commitment and perseverance are the keys to success.

REFERENCES

Epstein, Joyce, and Mac Iver, Douglas J. "National Practices and Trends in the Middle Grades." *Middle School Journal*, November 1990.

George, Paul, and Oldaker, Lynn. "A National Survey of Middle School Effectiveness." *Educational Leadership*, December 1985/January 1986.

Lounsbury, John H. "Less Is More in Middle School Scheduling." *Middle School Journal*, January 1981.

Mac Iver, Douglas J. "Meeting the Needs of Young Adolescents: Advisory Groups, Interdisciplinary Teams, and School Transition Programs." *Phi Delta Kappan*, February 1990.

Merenbloom, Elliot Y. *The Team Process: A Handbook for Teachers.* Columbus, Ohio: National Middle School Association, 1991.

Williamson, Ronald, and Johnston, J. Howard. *Planning for Success: Successful Implementation of Middle Level Reorganization.* Reston, Va.: National Association of Secondary School Principals, 1991.

4 School Transition Programs

MAKING the transition from elementary school to a middle level school can be stressful for many students. This change often includes not only a move away from an isolated neighborhood school to a larger, more diverse middle level school, but also a significant change in the structure and organization of the school day.

As middle level schools prepare for new students they often focus orientation programs on rules, regulations, and the organization of the school. However, these issues often do not hold the same significance for the middle level student that they do for adults.

Al Arth from the University of Nebraska—Lincoln conducted a multi-year study of student transition concerns. The study revealed that the primary concern of students entering the middle level school was "fear of failure," followed by worrying about drugs, giving a presentation in front of the class, being sent to the principal's office, being picked on, and dealing with unkind people.

In the Ann Arbor, Mich., public schools, like many other school districts, student orientation programs traditionally focused on the physical layout of the building, bus and lunchroom procedures, rules and regulations, and course selection. In 1987, in preparation for implementing a refined middle level program, the district surveyed students to determine the issues important to students during this transition. The most important issues for students were taking tests, taking showers in physical education, drugs, failure, giving presentations in front of the class, and changing clothes in physical education.

These or similar issues were of paramount importance to students, yet these topics were rarely if ever addressed in district student orientation or transition programs. Student input regarding the orientation/transition program is a necessary ingredient for success.

Planning the Process

Planning for a student orientation/transition program requires thoughtful information gathering as well as careful planning. To facilitate the planning for an orientation program, the middle level administrator may wish to consider several

,47, 4 36

key components: What is the rationale for a program? Who should participate in the activities? What will be included in the program? When should the process take place?

Rationale. Although there are many reasons to implement a comprehensive student orientation/transition program, the most important consideration should be the needs of students. A carefully implemented orientation program will help students make the transition to the middle level school by reducing anxiety, stress, and tension.

Simply describing how things will be at the new school and reciting rules and regulations is not sufficient. This may, in fact, increase student anxiety.

A transition program should also provide students and parents with information about the program at the middle level school, such as school organization and structure, course requirements and offerings, reporting and conferencing practices, activities programs, and student and parent organizations. This information provides students and parents with the opportunity to know what to expect at the middle level school and to receive information and clarification regarding practices and procedures.

The orientation program also helps middle level staff members gather data about the incoming students, such as their interests, concerns, and experiences. The orientation program provides the opportunity for the middle level staff members to build the first bridges to their new students.

Who. Middle level administrators have a primary role in facilitating the orientation/transition program. The relationship they establish with their colleagues at both the elementary and high school will help promote a climate conducive to meeting student needs.

The program must also involve other staff members, such as guidance staff, teachers, team leaders, and students. For example, at Marshall (Mich.) Middle School, incoming classes are paired with a current middle grades class during the orientation program. In addition to the pre-visit slide show and a question and answer session, the elementary and middle level teachers "team teach" for a day. This allows the students to become familiar with their new school and also models a collaborative and connected orientation program. This teaming arrangement also provides a mechanism for the elementary school staff to learn about the middle level program so they can provide ongoing support to students once they return to their elementary classrooms.

What. Decisions about what to include in a transition program are some of the most critical. The information shared with students and parents may either ease the transition or create barriers to success. Essential components of the program often include:
- Course requirements
- Typical schedules
- An orientation to the new school environment
- Discussion of cocurricular activities available to students.

In addition, a discussion of instructional practices used in the middle level school helps students and parents become at ease with the structure. A discussion of the teaming or advisory concept and its benefits for students is often helpful. Providing information about the exploratory program and its advantages for students will often alleviate concern about choices for students.

26

Another topic that helps support the transition is a discussion of the resources available to assist students. Counseling services, advisory programs, and student assistance programs are examples.

Students and parents will also want information about the cocurricular activities available in the school. Information about interscholastic and/or intramural programs, performing arts opportunities as well as clubs and other options for community service will be well received.

When. Effective transition programs are ongoing. Students are always in the process of making transitions and a sound practice is to provide multiple options for students to both gather and share information about those transitions.

Transition programs must be comprehensive enough to both provide needed information and not disrupt the routine of the sending program. They must assist with the transition, not hinder the process.

Where. Sound transition programs are the responsibility of both the sending and receiving schools. One effective way to demonstrate the connections between schools is to schedule activities at both the elementary and middle level schools. For example, middle level teachers and students might visit each elementary classroom to meet students, introduce themselves, and establish some initial links that might lead to a visit by the elementary students to the middle level school where they would be paired with the staff and students who visited their classroom.

Orientation Activities

The following activities represent the comprehensive nature of orientation programs:
- Produce a video for students about the middle level program
- Host parents' nights at the middle level school
- Make presentations in each individual elementary classroom
- Produce special editions of the school newspaper specifically for the incoming students
- Mail the middle level newsletter to the parents of incoming students
- Assign students to teams and advisory groups with at least one friend from elementary school
- Invite incoming students to participate in selected after-school activities in May
- Pair each elementary school classroom with a middle level class and have the students write letters to each other
- Create advisory or team groups in the spring and have middle level teachers send postcards or notes to each student in their incoming group during the summer
- Hold a scavenger hunt in the school during the orientation session so students can become familiar with the facility
- Have elementary school students shadow middle level students for a day
- Ask the middle school counselor to interview each elementary school student and send a follow-up letter to parents

- Conduct evening open houses during which the middle level students display their work or participate in performing groups
- Have students participate in a building trivia contest to familiarize themselves with the school and its facilities on opening day or during the orientation program.

Making a transition is not unlike the process of grieving. Students must be provided both time and opportunity to deal with the issues of change.

In this context, transition rituals take on added meaning. Terry Deal, in *Corporate Cultures*, describes these rituals as a means of letting go. Students must be given the opportunity to celebrate their accomplishments in their current school, recognize those who have assisted them, and look forward to the challenge and opportunity of the new school.

Course Selection

The course selection process provides a means to acquaint students and parents with the school's curricular and instructional program. Providing information about course offerings, course requirements, and the sequence of courses all enhance educational planning.

When preparing for course selection, middle level administrators should consider the format of the forms, support materials, and timelines.

1. *Format.* Selection materials should always be user-friendly. The format should be clear, concise, and easy to understand and use.
2. *Timelines.* When the schedule is developed, ample time should be provided to both convey the information to students and parents and allow them to process the information and make informed decisions. Allowing time for students and parents to discuss options often results in a more productive process. However, a final date for selecting courses must be set.
3. *Support Materials.* The development and distribution of supporting documents will help students and parents make decisions regarding courses. A course description guide, a list of course requirements for each grade of the school, and a suggested sequence of courses are examples of support documents that enhance the scheduling process.
4. *Other Information.* During the course selection process, parents and students also like to receive information about other components of a school's program. Details about student support services and the structure of the instructional program such as teaming or advisory programs may be pertinent to the selection of courses. For example, students may elect more challenging courses if they know a variety of academic and nonacademic supports are available.

Often the course selection process is the first contact parents and students have with a school. Attention to the details of the process benefits the school beyond simply gathering information about the choice of courses.

Summary

Orienting students to a new setting—either a new school or a new grade level—is an essential component of establishing a positive climate for students. Students approach times of transition with some trepidation. Activities that help them gain information and increase their comfort level are important factors in addressing this anxiety.

Assisting students with the transition process is the responsibility of everyone, not just the receiving school or the sending school. It is a shared responsibility between schools and a shared responsibility between the school and the home.

Transition programs are more than orientation. They are more than selecting courses. They are a reflection of the philosophy of the middle level school and its commitment to serving the needs of middle level students.

REFERENCES

Brazee, Edward. "Moving Into and Out of the Middle Level School." *Schools in the Middle*, April 1987.

Case, Andrew. "A Comprehensive Orientation Program for Incoming Sixth Graders." *Middle School Journal*, May 1989.

Epstein, Joyce, and Mac Iver, Douglas. *Education in the Middle Grades: National Practices and Trends*. Columbus, Ohio: National Middle School Association, 1990.

Glant, Lorna. "Moving to the Middle Without Misery." *Middle School Journal*, January 1989.

Mac Iver, Douglas J. "Meeting the Needs of Young Adolescents: Advisory Groups, Interdisciplinary Teaching Teams, and School Transition Programs." *Phi Delta Kappan*, February 1990.

Orlott, Charles. "The Rite of Safe Passage." *The Principal's Center Newsletter*, Harvard Graduate School of Education, Summer 1988.

Schurr, Sandra L. "Don't Just Welcome New Students—Meet and Greet Them!" *Middle School Journal*, May 1987.

Schwartz, Lester, and Corvasce, Fran. "The Buddy Program: A Peer Affective Education Program in the Middle School." *Middle School Journal*, May 1987.

Siehl, Peterann, and Gentry, Michael. "From Elementary to Middle School: Suggestions for a Comprehensive Orientation." *Middle School Journal*, January 1990.

Sportsman, Sally. "What Worries Kids About the Next Level." *Middle School Journal*, May 1987.

Toepfer, Conrad F. "Middle Level Transition and Articulation Issues." *Middle School Journal*, November 1986.

Vowels, Marty, and Rosa, Ann. "Helping Eighth Graders Make a Smooth Move." *Middle School Journal*, January 1989.

5   Staffing Considerations

STAFFING is one of the most important tasks associated with scheduling. The staffing process determines the courses offered, the number of sections of each course available, and, ultimately, the size of the staff and the number of students in each class.
Because of the critical impact of staffing, it is important to take special care to ensure the administrator plans carefully and follows procedural steps. Several important activities are vital in preparing for staffing decisions:

- Gathering information about staffing needs
- Establishing a timeline
- Generating staffing alternatives
- Selecting and placing staff.

Gathering Information

The key to successful staffing is gathering and organizing the information required for presentation to the personnel office. One important variable is student course selection. This selection should be finalized prior to making staffing decisions.

In many districts, the actual number of students electing a class is used to determine staffing levels. Therefore, if students have not indicated their enrollment for the following year, or have not returned the course selection forms, courses should be selected for them. This will ensure an allocation of staff to compensate for students who have not yet made selections.

Establishing a Timeline

While the procedure for allocating staff members varies among districts, the process generally involves the administrator meeting with a representative of the personnel office and the office of instruction to review building needs and anticipated staffing changes such as retirement, transfer, and leave. At this meeting or a subsequent session, the number of staff members allotted to the school will be determined.

It is important to establish a timeline for conducting this meeting and reaching agreement on staffing levels. It is often helpful for the middle level administrator to take the initiative and arrange for the meeting at an early date. Reaching an agreement about staffing decisions as early as possible provides more time to conduct the remainder of the scheduling activities before the end of the school year. This is particularly important if a goal of the scheduling process is to notify staff members of their assignments before they leave for the summer recess.

Preparing for Staffing

To prepare for staffing and scheduling decisions, administrators should have data such as a list of each course and the number of students electing each course, as well as the names of the students electing each course.

Most districts place some restrictions on course offerings. The most common restriction is that a minimum number of students must elect a course before it will be offered at the school. Other limits include restrictions on the number of staff members in a content area or the limits imposed by teaching stations in specialized areas such as technology education, computers, or art.

Once limits have been determined, it is important to review the information available to decide which courses will not be available. Students who selected these courses will need to be assigned to alternate classes. Adjusting selections will provide more accurate numbers on which to base staffing decisions.

Organizing the information required by the personnel office will make the staffing session more productive. The sample form included in Appendix C allows administrators to list each course in a content area and project the number of sections for each course. The number of projected sections can be approximated by dividing the total enrollment for the course by the maximum class size.

Most likely, the number of sections for each course is determined by the personnel office at the staffing session; however, in every case, the school should request the number of sections that will provide for the needs of the students of that school.

Prior to the staffing session, administrators should spend some time reviewing the needs of their students and enrollment levels, as well as staff qualifications and certification in order to assess staffing needs.

Additional thought might be given to the specific assignments for individual staff members. One strategy is to list the specific assignment anticipated for each staff person. This permits the administrator to have a picture of staff use. It also helps identify any known vacancies or needs that may need to be discussed with the personnel office.

Staffing Proposal

Teacher A:2—6th Grade Social Studies
      4—6th Grade Language Arts
Teacher B:3—7th Grade Math
      3—7th Grade Science
Teacher C:4—6th Grade Physical Education
      2—7th Grade Physical Education

Teacher D:3—Reading
      3—8th Grade English
Teacher E:5—7th Grade Science
      1—Science Coordinator
Teacher F:2—Computers
      2—7th Grade Math
      2—7th Grade Science

Selecting Staff Members

Teachers at the middle level are unique. They possess an irrepressible love of young adolescents, are sensitive to their changing development, and are committed to using instructional practices that are effective with early adolescents.

Middle level administrators are constantly in search of effective middle level teachers. Following the allocation of staff members, the administrator may have the opportunity to hire additional staff members either for newly allotted positions or to fill known vacancies.

J. Howard Johnston and Glenn Markle (1986) describe 18 "indicators of competency" in the behavior of middle level teachers. Based on extensive review of the literature, they determined that effective middle level teachers:
- Have a positive self-concept
- Demonstrate warmth
- Are optimistic
- Are enthusiastic
- Are flexible
- Are spontaneous
- Accept students
- Demonstrate awareness of developmental levels
- Demonstrate knowledge of subject matter
- Use a variety of instructional activities and materials
- Structure instruction
- Monitor learning
- Use concrete materials and focused learning strategies
- Ask varied questions
- Incorporate indirectness in teaching
- Incorporate "success-building" behavior in teaching
- Diagnose individual learning needs and prescribe individual instruction
- Listen.

These are desirable qualities in all teachers, but are particularly important at the middle level, where students exhibit such a wide range of development.

Placing Staff Members

The actual placement of staff members is one of the most important considerations in staffing the middle level school. Every state establishes specific requirements that affect staffing assignments. Local districts, often through the collective bargaining process, identify additional staffing parameters, such as teaching within majors or minors, transfer procedures, and seniority requirements.

In addition to these state and local requirements, middle level administrators must consider other factors in staffing their school. The most important consideration is ensuring that the staff members are selected and placed so the curricular and instructional programs are positively affected. At the middle level, consideration should be given to ensuring that teaching teams are balanced regarding teaching speciality and teaching style. However, first and foremost, the middle level teacher must enjoy the challenges and rewards of working with early adolescents.

In assigning staff members, the middle level administrator should be as responsive to the staff members as possible. While it is not always possible to place all staff members in the assignment of their choice, the middle level program is enhanced when there is a match between the teacher's strengths and skills and the assignment.

Disagreements will arise, but it is important to use good personnel practices in resolving the issues. Utilizing effective listening skills, working collaboratively toward the resolution of differences, and explaining reasons for decisions are important.

Summary

The schedule of a middle level school is enhanced by the appropriate selection and placement of staff. Effective middle level teachers exhibit special characteristics. Attention to matching teacher skills with the needs of the instructional program will ensure that the full potential of the school schedule is achieved.

REFERENCES

Johnston, J. Howard, and Markle, Glenn C. *What Research Says to the Middle Level Practitioner*. Columbus, Ohio: National Middle School Association, 1986.

6 Preparing To Schedule

ONCE student course selection is finalized and staffing decisions have been made, the final steps can be taken to prepare the schedule. Those steps include adjusting course selections, determining staff preferences, and creating advisory groups/teams.

Adjusting Course Selections

As a result of the staffing process, it is likely that several courses that had been planned will not be offered. Students who selected those classes will need to be scheduled into alternate selections. These alternate selections must be placed in the data file if a data system is used for scheduling.

These changes result in modified tallies for each course, so administrators should verify that sufficient sections of each course will be available.

Determining Staff Preferences

At this time it is useful to ask staff members whether they have any preferences regarding their assignments. In states with collective bargaining, this process may be required according to provisions in the teachers' contract. In all cases, this information allows the staff members to be involved in determining their assignments and often improves school climate.

Creating Advisory Groups/Teams

In schools with an advisory program and/or interdisciplinary teams, one of the most complicated yet most critical activities of the scheduling process is the grouping of students. The development of these student groups is an essential component of implementing and enhancing the basic mission of the middle level school and becomes a visible expression of the school's philosophy.

Establishing these student groups early in the scheduling process is critical, as it will both ease and simplify subsequent tasks.

To establish the groups, the administrator needs the following information about each student: gender and ethnic status, feeder school, skill level, and special needs such as reading, special education, or English as a second language. The school's criteria for placing students must be available and well-articulated.

The goal should be to create advisory or team groupings that are heterogeneous and closely approximate the student population of that grade. However, the policy in some districts and the law in some states requires that some classes be grouped based on student achievement levels—usually in the areas of special education and gifted and talented. If this is the case, these requirements serve as another factor in preparing the student groups.

Once administrators have gathered the required information, they can begin to group students. Some data systems provide an option for arranging these groups. Most often this is a manual process that permits the middle level administrator to be flexible and responsive to student needs. Regardless of the grouping process, several steps may be followed to ease the process.

Once the number of groups has been determined, the administrator should determine the number of students in each group based on the various criteria (ethnic, gender, skill level, special needs, feeder schools, etc.). One method is illustrated in Figure 1. This form provides a handy reference for ensuring that the classroom groups are balanced based on the agreed-to criteria.

FIGURE 1

CLASSROOM GROUPING

Student Name	M/F	Ethnic	Special Needs	Feeder School	Ach. Level	Comments

Once the classroom groups are developed, the administrator is ready to assign course numbers.

Computer or No Computer

Administrators may often choose whether or not to use a data system when preparing a schedule. Options include using a manual system, participating in a district or consortium data system, or utilizing a microcomputer. Even within these options there are additional considerations. For example, the administrator may use a computer to build the schedule or manually build the schedule and then use the computer to schedule students.

There are advantages and disadvantages to all scheduling methods. The key consideration is the degree of control the administrator wants over the final product. It is always important to focus on developing a schedule that facilitates the instructional program and enhances the ability of students to take the courses they want.

Perhaps the most common scheduling system is to mix the use of a manual system with the advantages of a data system. For example, a computer system is used to tabulate and generate data about student course selections. The administrator manually creates the schedule, then uses the computer to place students into classes by simulating student schedules. Once the administrator is satisfied with the schedule, he or she uses the computer to generate student schedules, class lists, and other reports.

Before selecting a computer software system, administrators should consider several key questions. These questions, published by the Michigan Association of Secondary School Principals, are included in Appendix E. The list was developed by Robert Schramke, principal of Redford (Mich.) Union High School.

Regardless of the system selected, there are several common elements in preparing to schedule:

1. Determining any curricular or instructional parameters or guidelines such as grouping practices or teaming arrangements
2. Preparing materials and establishing timelines
3. Gathering information from students
4. Determining staff needs
5. Building the schedule
6. Refining the schedule.

In most software packages, one of the most difficult tasks is scheduling students onto teams with blocks of time without the computer totally confusing the composition of the student groups.

One strategy is to utilize the strength of the computer process by creating a series of special course numbers or singleton courses to force the computer to maintain the integrity of the student groups. These numbers are used for no purpose other than to schedule all students on a team with the same group of teachers. The use of singleton course numbers ensures that each course, or group of students, is unique.

Figure 2 provides an example of this process.

Each team is assigned the special numbers for the classes that all students attend. In the example, those classes are language arts, mathematics, science, and social studies.

The next step is critical if a data system is being utilized. All students in the group must have their selections changed from the course numbers on the data system to the special numbers being used. Once the special numbers are entered, the administrator uses them to build the master schedule on the data system. This allows only students on a particular team to be assigned to the sections of courses taught by the team teachers.

FIGURE 2

7TH GRADE TEAM:

A team of four teachers (language arts, math, science and social studies) working with four groups of students.

Group	Course	Special Course Number
Student Group A:	Language Arts	141
	Mathematics	341
	Science	441
	Social Studies	241
Student Group B:	Language Arts	142
	Mathematics	342
	Science	442
	Social Studies	242
Student Group C:	Language Arts	143
	Mathematics	343
	Science	443
	Social Studies	243
Student Group D:	Language Arts	144
	Mathematics	344
	Science	444
	Social Studies	244

Once the data are entered, the administrator may request a listing of students sorted on particular team course numbers. This provides a list of each team class and allows the administrator to verify student placement. It also facilitates any adjustments that may be needed to ensure balance across teams and/or advisory groups.

Remember, the data system will assign students to classes based on the information in the computer file. If the data are not correct, students will not be placed in the classes they desire.

Reviewing the Priorities

Before going further, the administrator developing the specifics of the schedule should review the school goals and priorities. Adjustments in the priorities may be needed. If so, this is the time to make the modifications. The schedule should be a means to achieve the school's mission and goals.

Summary

Preparing for the actual scheduling is a critical step. Essential components of this planning include encouraging staff input, modifying student course selections to reflect actual courses being offered, and creating team and advisory groups.

7 Building a Block-Time Schedule

AFTER gathering a base of information, delineating scheduling parameters, and thinking about the nature of the schedule, the next step is to actually begin to place teams, advisory groups, and blocks of time into a workable schedule.

Scheduling a middle level school requires addressing the mythology of school scheduling. Dispelling some of these myths will help middle level administrators design and implement a sound school schedule.

Myth #1—Schedules are interchangeable. Just as no two classrooms are alike, no two middle level schools are identical. The obvious characteristics such as enrollment and physical plant affect the structure of a school schedule. Enrollment determines staffing levels and the comprehensiveness of the program, while the physical plant influences the school's ability to respond to needs for flexible space and adjacent classrooms. Most middle level school buildings were not designed around the middle level concept and this limits the flexibility of building use.

More important, each school serves a unique set of students with their own characteristics and needs; a unique set of teachers, some of whom are strong advocates of the middle level concept, and some who are not; and a unique school community.

Each of these factors influences the nature of the middle level program and thus the structure of the schedule. A schedule that works well at one site may not be appropriate in another location.

Myth #2—Everyone will love a flexible schedule. Every school has staff members who oppose every initiative. They will also oppose a flexible schedule. The flexible schedule requires that staff members assume roles they may not have experienced. It will require communication with colleagues on a team, advance planning, and thoughtful deliberation about the needs of both the students and the curriculum.

Middle level administrators must provide staff members with the opportunity to learn about the new structure, talk about its implementation, and work with colleagues to develop the skills necessary for successful implementation. The challenge is to keep the focus on addressing the needs of students rather that ensuring the comfort level of the staff.

Myth #3—Flexible scheduling is less work. Implementing flexible scheduling requires teachers to interact with their colleagues in nontraditional ways. This interaction around both curricular issues and the use of blocks of time can require additional time for discussion and planning and create interpersonal conflicts that may require resolution.

A flexible schedule may significantly alter the way a staff does business with students. Teachers will need to review the allotment of time and make decisions regarding the interrelationship of the curriculum. Maintaining the focus on students and their needs will result in a program that offers hope for both improved student achievement and improved attitudes about school.

Myth #4—All blocks of time and schedules must be alike. Just as every middle level student is unique, so are the teams of teachers working with the students. The power of a flexible schedule is the ability of a teaching team to respond to the needs of students. The needs of sixth graders differ from the needs of eighth graders. The strengths of one team will differ from those of another. The schedule's responsiveness to student needs is a major indicator of the strength of the overall middle level program.

Locating the Blocks

A necessary step in developing a block-time schedule is determining the location of the various blocks. In making this decision, several variables must be considered:
- Length of individual blocks
- Number of teams scheduled for blocks
- Room availability
- Lunch schedules
- Teacher workload constraints
- Elective course offerings
- Singleton courses available to students in more than one grade.

To assist with this planning, it might be useful to consider a format similar to that in Figure 1. This chart permits the middle level administrator to place individual blocks onto a schedule, to identify when certain specific courses will meet, and to note issues yet to be resolved. This visual look at the schedule, location of blocks, and the way in which they interrelate will help the administrator clarify adjustments that must be made to the schedule.

In the example, blocks of time are scheduled for all three grades in the school. In addition, at each grade level there are both morning and afternoon blocks. During the second class period, all grades are in academic blocks. This model permits all elective teachers to have this class period for common planning. However, in many schools such a schedule would not be possible due to insufficient classrooms.

The example illustrates when certain singleton courses will be offered. Seventh and eighth grade band must be fourth hour when neither grade is in the block, and the first year of foreign language, available only to eighth graders, must be either third or fifth hour when eighth graders may be in electives. Foreign language should

Figure 1

MIDDLE SCHOOLS

	Sixth	Seventh	Eighth
1	Block		Block
2	Block	Block	Block
3		Block	
4	Block		
5	Block	Block	
6		Block	Block
7			Block

COURSE	HOUR	COMMON PLANNING TIME		ISSUES TO BE RESOLVED
Band 7 & 8	4	All 6th Acad. Staff	3, 6	Lunch Schedules
For. Lang. 1	3 or 5	All 7th Acad. Staff	1, 4	Exploratory Rotation
		All 8th Acad. Staff	4, 5	
		Elective Staff	2	

not be scheduled during fourth hour due to the high probability that students in foreign language will also be in band.

This example illustrates the benefits of doing preliminary planning. The identification of appropriate times for blocks, their location, and potential conflicts will assist the middle level administrator in developing a successful schedule.

Simulations

After establishing school priorities, delineating staffing levels, and gathering information from and about students and staff members, the administrator can develop the specifics of the schedule. Many middle level administrators do several scheduling simulations on paper. Simulations assist in determining the location of blocks of time for teams and the placement of courses offered in a particular curricular area.

The simulation process permits a review of individual pieces of the schedule without using the data system. This simulation process often provides insights that help smooth the scheduling process later in the year.

During this phase of scheduling it is also useful to develop a clear idea of the specific staff assignments. For example, Teacher A may teach three sections of world geography, two sections of language arts, and be a teacher adviser. Teacher B may be assigned two classes in communication skills, one class in beginning theatre, and two classes of performing arts.

41

Detailing the assignment of each staff member gives the administrator a picture of the way each assignment will be structured. It will also help identify any staffing needs.

It is best not to notify teachers of their specific assignment prior to constructing the actual master schedule. As the schedule evolves it may be necessary to adjust specific staff assignments so that a greater number of students may access the classes they elected. Early notification may reduce some of the flexibility available to the administrator and impede development of a sound schedule.

Building the Schedule

Before building the schedule, administrators should consider several factors that affect the process.
- The schedule of part-time teachers
- Common planning time needs
- Teaming arrangements
- Lunch considerations and the impact on classes that include students from more than one grade
- Teaching stations in such areas as music, home economics, art, and technology education
- Contractual limits on the number of preparations and assignments.

A closer look at some of these issues will provide insights into their specific impact on development of a school schedule.

Program Issues. Several factors are involved in this component, including grouping (heterogeneous or homogeneous); course requirements; support programs such as special education, Chapter 1, and English as a second language; and contractual issues related to teacher workload.

Teaming Issues. Teaming is so closely related to the concept of flexible scheduling that it is essential to consider the structure of a school's teaming program. Issues such as the size of teams, the length of blocks, grouping issues, teacher certification, common planning time, and a common block of instructional time must be addressed.

Physical Space. The physical layout of the school will affect both the nature of the program and the structure of the schedule. For example:
- Is it possible for team members to be located in adjacent classrooms?
- Does the departmental structure of the school lend itself to a teaming arrangement?
- Do staff members have a vested interest in maintaining their classrooms in certain locations within the school?
- Is the school building large enough to provide both large group and small group instructional space?
- Are there adequate facilities for team planning? .

Either on paper, a magnetic board, chalkboard, or other device, the administrator should begin to place individual sections of classes into the schedule. This permits early adjustment of courses to avoid later conflicts.

Singletons and Doubletons

Administrators must consider the location of singletons and doubletons. Singletons are courses that meet only once during the school day; doubletons meet twice. These courses may conflict with many other courses because there are only one or two opportunities for a student to take each course. If a student elects to take two singleton courses and those courses are scheduled during the same class period, there will be a conflict that must be resolved.

Avoid conflicts when the schedule is initially built. For example, if it is probable that students taking band and orchestra will also take foreign language, scheduling these two classes during the same period will likely create conflicts. However, scheduling French 1 and Spanish 1 during the same period would have few if any conflicts, since few students elect more than one foreign language.

If a data system is utilized for scheduling, a conflict matrix report will be useful in identifying the potential conflicts between singleton and doubleton courses. A sample conflict matrix is included in Appendix D.

When using a manual scheduling system, it is also important to gather data regarding potential conflicts. This data can be tallied by reviewing student course selection sheets and tabulating the number of students electing certain other courses. Limiting the number of courses reviewed will simplify the process.

Building the Specifics

After tentatively placing every section of every course into the schedule, the administrator should review each class hour to ensure balance in the variety of classes offered and the varied skill level of courses, and to ensure that a sufficient number of sections are available to accommodate the students in each grade. Attention to these details at this stage will preclude major restructuring of the schedule later.

As soon as balance in the schedule has been achieved, the middle level administrator should build the specifics of the schedule. If the administrator is using a data system, this will include entering each individual section into the system. The administrator should provide all the necessary detail, such as room numbers and section codes. It is easy to defer assigning these data until a later date, but the further along the process, the more difficult it becomes to adjust courses and rooms.

Strategies for Manipulating the Schedule

Every student must be able to participate in every aspect of the school program. In reality, however, every schedule will include conflicts. The goal of most scheduling processes is to reduce the number of conflicts and to improve every year's schedule based on the experience of the previous year. Striking a balance between individual student needs and the need to reduce conflicts is at the heart of the scheduling task.

Perhaps the greatest variable affecting the middle level schedule is the length of the school day. Starting and ending times are generally regulated by transportation schedules and definitions of workload included in labor agreements. The number of minutes in each school day is finite. Therefore, the challenge confronting the middle level administrator is to manipulate the use of those minutes to ensure a program that responds to students.

The following are strategies that may be used to address scheduling issues.

1. Challenge the Regularities. The middle level administrator may need to challenge some of the givens in a school day to build flexibility into the schedule.

- Do all classes need to meet every day?
- Do all class periods need to be of a uniform length?
- Does a school need to have class periods and bell schedules?
- Does every day have to have the same number of class periods?
- Does every teacher need to work with students from only a single grade?

The answers to these and others will determine the structure of the school schedule. For example, some courses may meet on an alternating day basis. Perhaps a school can use a drop schedule and schedule eight classes over a seven-period day. Using blocks of time will provide flexibility for teams to restructure instructional time. Bells may be a hindrance to the concept of blocks of time.

2. Focus on Middle Level Students. Often the high school program will affect the middle level school. This may be due to transportation schedules or the use of staff members shared between the two levels. If so, administrators may need to negotiate with the personnel office about the use of staff members, negotiate with the high school administrators regarding scheduling of staff members, or work with the central office to adjust transportation schedules.

Staff use is one of the critical variables in a master schedule. The administrator must be willing to convert existing teaching positions to a different use, review teacher certification and past experience to determine the flexibility of staff to assume modified positions, talk to staff members about taking a different role in the school, and discuss with the personnel office or the administrators of other schools the flexibility to trade teachers or convert vacancies into other positions.

3. Adjust Placement of Blocks. Be creative in manipulating the major variables of the school day. Perhaps varying the length of the blocks or adjusting their location in the day will facilitate the schedule. Blocks of three or four class periods may greatly enhance the instructional program and might be advantageous to students and teachers.

All teams within a given grade may not need to have the same schedule, but to maintain team integrity, it is important that all team members have a similar schedule and common planning time. All teams may not require the same schedule. Such adjustments may enhance the ability to offer electives to students in more than one grade or to access the exploratory or elective program. However, such a shift might also hinder the schedule by inhibiting cross-team communication, requiring inappropriate grouping of students, or restricting student access to the full range of elective courses.

4. Value Collaboration. Involving the staff and students in schedule development can greatly expand the perspectives about the schedule and provide insights that will improve it. Guidance and clerical staff often have valuable knowledge about the functioning of the schedule and its impact on students. For example, the guidance secretary will know which courses are creating conflicts for students based on student requests. The secretary will also have developed some thoughts about potential solutions to the conflicts. Tapping these resources will lead to a better product.

Students also have opinions about the impact of the schedule on their life. For example, at one middle school students have three lunch periods. The lunch periods include students from all three grades at the school. Due to the structure of the teaching teams, students at any grade level have little opportunity to interact with other students at that same grade. This was an issue of major importance to the student body and one that could be addressed by modifying the schedule. Certainly, such attention to student needs promotes a climate of greater respect and builds support and ownership for the scheduling model.

Summary

Implementing a block-time schedule often complicates the scheduling process by reducing some of the flexibility available to the administrator. Determining the length and location of the instructional blocks and the preferred combination of blocks can be a particular challenge. Middle level administrators can schedule nearly anything, they just can't schedule everything—particularly in the same schedule.

Analyzing the school schedule and adjusting the variables based upon established priorities is the key to successful scheduling. Striving for flexibility and a structure that enhances student learning is a worthy effort and one that the middle level administrator will eagerly accept.

8 Refining the Schedule

AFTER the schedule is created, administrators should review the reports detailing the degree to which students were successfully scheduled.

Attention to several items will assist with this process:

- Obtain reports detailing all students who did not receive all their requests, schedules that have conflicts, and noted errors
- Enter course selections for any newly enrolled students
- Verify that course selections have been altered for students who elected courses that will not be included in the schedule
- Ensure that course selections have been modified for any student for whom you have used a special number.

Developing a schedule entails systematically adjusting both the schedule of classes and the selections made by students. The priority should always be adjusting the schedule to maximize student access to the curriculum. Occasionally, however, changes in student selections are necessary.

When adjustments must be made in the schedule there are several options available to the administrator. They include:

- Moving a section of a class to a different class period
- Adjusting the number of seats available for students in a given class
- Modifying the course selections made by the student
- Changing the room number or teacher for a course section.

Remember, as soon as one class section is moved to a different location in the schedule, all data about conflicts and other scheduling problems are no longer valid. The administrator should always think carefully about the implications of all schedule adjustments. However, adjustments must be made.

After reviewing all scheduling reports and making the necessary adjustments to the schedule, the administrator should request the use of an additional simulation to schedule students. Reviewing reports, making adjustments, and requesting a schedule may be repeated as often as the time schedule permits or until it is clear that further adjustment will no longer improve the quality of the schedule for students.

Some students will have "irresolvable" conflicts. The nature of a schedule is such that some students will require combinations of courses that just don't fit together in the schedule. This may be due to the selection of a large number of singleton or doubleton courses, or just the combination of courses selected.

When adjusting the schedule will not help resolve a student conflict, the guidance staff can review the course selections and work with both the student and her or his parents to modify the selections. Be assured that not every student is able to receive every course selected. There always reaches a point where some "irresolvables" remain.

The schedule may be adjusted until the administrator is satisfied that further adjustment will not assist students in accessing the curriculum. When that point is reached, the administrator should consult with the data center about next steps in finalizing the schedule and arrange for the opening of school.

Before moving ahead, the middle level administrator should be able to answer several questions affirmatively.

- Is the number of students receiving all requests greater than 85 percent?
- Are there fewer than five "irresolvables"?
- Have student course selections been adjusted to resolve "irresolvables"?
- Do reports from the data center indicate that all courses are scheduled into class periods that serve the maximum number of students?
- Are you satisfied that you have been sufficiently flexible in adjusting the schedule to meet the needs of your middle level students?

At this point in scheduling it is important to have a copy of each student's schedule. Then, a member of the staff—clerical, administrative, or guidance—may wish to review each schedule to ensure that every student has a complete schedule. Adjustments should be made to either add classes or resolve conflicts for students prior to the opening of school.

There are two major benefits to taking the time for these adjustments prior to the beginning of school. First, middle level students are often anxious and apprehensive at the start of a year. Receiving a schedule that has blanks, gaps, or missing parts often exacerbates this anxiety. Second, every scheduling problem will need to be resolved at some point. Addressing the issue early on will make the beginning of the year less frantic for students, parents, and school staff.

Summary

There is no perfect schedule; there are many excellent schedules. Refining a schedule is based on the belief that the schedule should be a reflection of the middle level school's priority to serve students. The inclusion of flexible options and strategies for ensuring that all students have equal access to the school's program are important components of a middle level schedule.

9 Opening School

CONGRATULATIONS! School is about to begin and you have completed the final steps in the scheduling process. Prior to the opening of school some final things must be done to prepare the schedule.

New Students

During the summer, students move away and new students enroll in their place. This dynamic nature of schools can have a positive impact on the program, but it can also affect both the structure and the organization of a school schedule.

New students rarely take the same classes as those who moved. This means that even the most perfect schedules will require adjustment. As new students are placed in teams and advisory groups, middle level administrators will want to ensure balance in the groups based on the criteria used to initially form them.

The first step is to review the class roster for each group, deleting the names of all students who have left the school. Tallies should then be made of the remaining students with regard to gender, ethnic group, achievement, and total number of students in each group. Then, all newly enrolled students should be placed into the groups to maintain the demographic balance.

Reports and Schedules

It is important to request all the reports necessary to open school, including copies of student schedules, class lists, and copies of the master schedule. Back-up copies of student schedules and class lists for teachers should be available.

Clerical, guidance, and administrative staff members should have copies of all reports so they may monitor students, make appropriate adjustments, and share information with students and parents.

Starting School

In the rush to begin the school year it is easy to lose sight of the many positives achieved by the schedule. Some students and parents will be displeased and some staff members will criticize the structure of the schedule. However, displeasure for some seems to be the hallmark of any school schedule. Remember, there are no perfect schedules!

The middle level administrator should not discount or brush aside reaction to or feedback regarding the schedule. Every schedule can be improved, and the beginning of the year is as an appropriate time to gather input from constituent groups about the schedule.

Perhaps the groups most aware of the impact of the entire schedule will be the guidance and clerical staff. Many administrators schedule time to meet with guidance and clerical personnel to discuss the schedule, identify areas of concern, and solicit suggestions for ways to modify and strengthen the schedule for the coming year. Maintaining a collective memory regarding the schedule will be very useful when it is time to begin the process again.

Summary

As the school year gets under way, middle level administrators should congratulate themselves on completing one of the most rigorous activities of the school year—completing the master schedule. The schedule affects every phase of a school's operation and can either facilitate or hinder the school's program.

Developing and implementing a flexible schedule—one that takes into account the developmental needs of middle level students and offers opportunities for addressing those needs—is a challenge. However, it is a challenge worth undertaking and one on which the middle level administrator will want to persevere. It serves students well and that is the mission of the middle level school.

Appendix A
Scheduling Timeline

Each s   a timeline of scheduling activities based on local
parameter   example illustrates many of the items you
may wish

Date	Activity
Jan 10	Obtain est...
Jan 15	Prepare information for data p..
	Consult with elementary principals regarding ... ntation/course selection process.
Jan 30	Meet with staff to develop and review course selection materials, orientation activities.
Feb	Prepare course selection materials.
	Gather data regarding students (gender, ethnic, achievement, special services).
Feb 15	Meet with high school staff to develop transition activities.
	Distribute course selection materials.
Feb 20	Conduct parent orientation meetings.
Mar 1	Conduct student orientation meetings.
	High school counselors visit.
Mar 15	9th grade course selection materials returned to high school.
Mar 20	Deadline for 6th, 7th, and 8th grade course selection materials
	• counselors edit, update, and correct
	• secretaries enter into data system.
Mar 30	Course selection sheets to data processing.
Apr 1	High school counselors visit to review course selection materials.
Apr 5	Course selection tallies available from data.
Apr 15	Staffing levels determined in conjunction with personnel office.
May 1	Preliminary master schedule developed.
May 10- June 1	Edit master schedule/conduct scheduling simulations.
May 20	Fifth graders visit.
June 1- June 15	Counselors resolve scheduling conflicts.
June 20	Receive preliminary class lists and schedules.
	Finalize schedule on data system.
Aug 15	Adjust schedule based on summer changes.
	Schedule newly enrolled students.
	Request class lists and schedules.

Appendix B
Letter to Staff

The following memo was prepared by a Michigan middle level principal describing the considerations in developing a master schedule.

TO: Staff
DATE: April 12, 1990
RE: Master Schedule

Yesterday's discussion at staff meeting regarding the master schedule was cut short because some had to get to a 4:45 p.m. meeting. But there seems to be a great deal of interest in how the master schedule "comes together," and the parameters for developing the schedule. So, if anyone is interested, here are all of the parameters. They are listed in no particular order. If you want to have a go at it, please do. Let me know if you come up with anything we can consider.

Time Parameters

- Begin at 8:05 a.m., end at 2:45
- Twenty-five minute advisory
- Seven 45-minute classes
- Five-minute passing times
- Three lunch periods, 30 minutes portal to portal (from the time one class ends until the next begins)
- Twenty minutes between lunches

Other Parameters

- Block time for academics
- Two orchestras must be scheduled back-to-back
- 7th and 8th graders must have two common elective periods to accommodate singleton electives open to both grades
- Common planning time for teams
- Common planning time for electives
- No more than three sections of phys. ed. in any class period
- Foreign language does not meet at same time as music at the same grade level
- 6th grade exploratory—12 sections equal three strands; must be back-to-back to accommodate shared teachers
- During exploratory hour, all 7th and 8th graders must be in academics because all elective teachers are busy
- No 7th or 8th grade instrumental music can meet during 6th period because music teachers are scheduled for other classes
- Each hour there must be 617 seats available (221 for sixth, 206 for seventh, 190 for eighth)

- No teacher can teach more than 200 minutes in a row without a lunch break or planning time
- Part-time teachers, unless they are full-time in the district, must have their teaching assignments back-to-back since they do not receive planning time
- No more than two-thirds of the students may be in electives at any one time because there are not enough classes to accommodate them
- Be careful during lunch times; it's easy to overlook the fact that hours become staggered and assign teachers to overlapping classes
- If advisory is not at the beginning of the day, be careful where you put lunch
- Full-time teachers must have five assignments

I'm pretty sure those are all the things that have to be worked with. I hope I haven't missed any, because if any of you spend much time trying to draw up some skeleton master schedules only to find I've overlooked some critical element(s), you'll not be happy with me. Since I'm writing this at one o'clock in the morning, though, I can't promise I've thought of everything.

If you like puzzles, this task is for you. It's fun, actually—just very frustrating.

Appendix C
Determining Staffing Levels

When determining staffing levels it is often helpful to know how many students are electing each course. This format might help gather this information and help determine the number of sections to offer.

PROJECTED COURSE ENROLLMENTS

School _____   School Year _____

Department _____   Semester _____

Course Number	Course Title	Proj. Enroll.	Proj. Sect.	Avg. Size

Total Sections _____   Dept. Staff F.T.E. _____

Appendix D
Conflict Matrix

A matrix is generated by most data systems or may be constructed manually. The information helps administrators schedule classes when there will be the fewest conflicts. For example, on this matrix, scheduling Course 710 would create 24 conflicts if scheduled at the same time as Course 812.

Course	Requests	Leisure Arts 806 14	Choices 807 26	Expl w/Comp 812 63	Alg 8 851 23	Alg 8 852 11	Alg 8 853 8	Alg 8 854 23	Comm Tech 902 42	Manuf Tech 904 73	Const Tech 905 62	Transp T 906 21
512 Spanish 1B	25			1	5	3		6		4	5	1
513 Spanish 1	25			2	4	3	1	5		1	6	1
603 Orchestra 6A	15											
604 Band 6A	35							1				
607 Beg Inst 7/8	11	1			1		1	1		2		
610 Ms Singers	12			1	1	1						
611 Mixed Choir	14	1		1	1		1	1		1	2	
612 Con Orchestr	12			4	1	1		1		2	1	
614 7/8 Band I	52		4	5	9	4	3	7	4	3	6	3
702 Draw/Print	77	6	6	18	5	3	1	5	8	23	25	11
703 Paint/Comp	44	2	5	10	4	3	3	3	4	12	9	4
704 Des Nature	36	1	9	18					5	8	4	3
705 Art In Env	19	4	4	2	1		1	5		9	6	3
706 Applied Art	51	5	7	10	5	1	2	6	6	26	14	5
707 Cer/Sculp	92	2	5	16	2	5	3	6	11	19	17	6
710 Key/W Pro IA	88	4	11	24	6	5	3	2	10	28	21	5
711 Key/W Pro IB	32	1	3	4	9	2	2	3		11	9	1
760 Expl Arts	152			1						21		
761 Expl Arts	155			1						21		
802 Food Life I	133	9	9	27	7	2	3	6	8	24	23	2

Appendix E
Factors To Consider in Selecting
A Scheduling Program

Administrative Factors:

1. Does the program have the ability to be accessed by counselors, secretaries, and administrators?

2. Can the computer generate its own forms for report cards?

3. Do you depend on the vendor to supply you with report forms or report cards?

4. Are data stored in a form that a programmer in your building can easily retrieve and update?

5. Can data be imported/exported if you decide to change systems?

6. Can data be downloaded from your present system?

7. Is the system totally integrated (i.e., are attendance and grade reporting included at this time, or can they be added at a future date)?

8. Does the software have the ability to provide access for various input devices such as Scantron or a bar code system?

9. Is the system user-friendly?

10. Can people be trained and re-trained to operate the software?

11. Does it further the effort to make counseling paper-and-pencil-free prior to the first tally?

12. Is a security system built into the program?

Scheduling Functions:

1. Does the program have an automatic master schedule builder as part of the scheduling procedure?

2. Does the software have the capability to automatically schedule a new student when the student arrives at your school (auto scheduler)?

3. When a schedule is created for a new student, is a copy immediately available?

4. Can a student be manually scheduled?

5. Can students be globally scheduled for classes?

6. Can maximum and minimum class sizes be controlled/adjusted?

7. Can the program identify specific courses as a priority?

8. Can multiple hour classes be scheduled? Two-hour blocks? Three-hour blocks? Four-hour blocks?

9. Can the program handle less than semester classes, such as nine-week or trimester classes?

10. How long does it take to complete a schedule run?

11. Is room management possible?

12. Is it possible to link courses?

13. Can an updated master file be printed at any time?

14. Can schedules, attendance, and transcript records be viewed on a CRT at any time?

15. Can you print screen information?

16. Can a conflict matrix be generated for selected singleton, doubleton courses?

17. Can pre-scheduling class lists be generated from the tally?

Hardware:

1. What type of hardware is required? Can scheduling software run on the current computer system and other future systems?

2. Does your hardware support the software system?

3. Will software run on all major operating systems, for example MS-DOS and UNIX?

Software Company:

1. How many schools/references are provided?

2. How long has the software company been in business?

3. How long has the company supported this particular program?

4. What kind of phone support do you have? (Can a modem be used to send problem data analysis?)

5. What is the length and type of training required?

Cost Factors:

1. What is the total cost of the system?

2. Does the support service cost more than 10–15 percent of the purchase price each year?

3. Is there a cost when the system is updated?

Reprinted with permission from:
Michigan Association of Secondary School Principals and Robert Schramke, Principal of Redford Union High School, Redford, Mich.